THIS CANDLEWICK BOOK BELONGS TO:

_____

_____

_____

_____

The park is dark,
The monsters thin,
It's feeding time
So COME ON IN!

For Louis Patrick Lawrence Cornelius Monahan

Second U.S. paperback edition 2002

The Library of Congress has cataloged the hardcover edition as follows:

McNaughton, Colin.
Making friends with Frankenstein ; a book of monstrous poems
and pictures / Colin McNaughton. —1st U.S. ed.
Summary: Presents a collection of silly, scary, and disgusting poems
about monsters and other unusual creatures.
ISBN 1-56402-308-7 (hardcover)
ISBN 1-56402-962-X (large paperback 1st edition)
ISBN 0-7636-1552-8 (paperback)
1. Monsters—Juvenile poetry. 2. Children's poetry, English.
[1. Monsters—Poetry. 2. English poetry.] I. Title.
PR6063.C65M34   1994
821'.914—dc20   93-20027

ISBN 0-7636-1891-8 (large paperback 2nd edition)

Printed in Hong Kong

This book was typeset in Caslon 540.
The illustrations were done in watercolor.

Candlewick Press
2067 Massachusetts Avenue
Cambridge, Massachusetts 02140

visit us at www.candlewick.com

MaKing FrieNDS WiTH FRANKENSTEiN

A Book of Monstrous Poems and Pictures

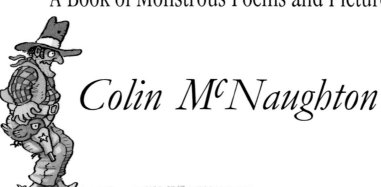

Colin McNaughton

CANDLEWICK PRESS
CAMBRIDGE, MASSACHUSETTS

COCKROACH SANDWICH

Cockroach sandwich
For my lunch,
Hate the taste
But love the crunch!

WE'RE HAVING A MONSTER PARTY!

We're having a monster party;
    We're having a monster crowd.
We're having a monster singsong
    And the music is monster LOUD!

We're doing a monster shimmy;
    We're turning a-monster-round.
We're doing a monster shuffle
    And we're making a monster sound!

Lardy, lardy, squiggly woo,
    Do the monster BUMP!
Linky, lanky, diddly doo,
    Do the monster JUMP!

Widdly, waddly, kink-a-joo,
    Sing the monster SONG!
Diddly, doddly, stinky-poo,
    Bang the monster GONG!

Bang, bang, tickety-boo,
  Do the monster SHAKE!
Clang, clang, flickety-goo,
  Make the building QUAKE!

Yes, we're having a monster party,
  The best you've monster seen!
It's the biggest monster party
  That there's ever monster been!

GEORGIE PORGIE

Georgie Porgie's been so bad —
Kissed the girls and made them mad.
When the boys came out to play —
The ambulance took George away!

TEACHER'S PET

Call a doctor,
Call the vet!
I've just been bitten
By teacher's pet!

BULLY BOY McCOY

I'm Bully Boy McCoy, ahoy!
An' bein' a bully's what I enjoy!
   I'll bully thee,
   If yer smaller'n me,
I'm Bully Boy McCoy, ahoy!

I'm Bully Boy McCoy, avast!
Hand o'er yer treasure an' make it fast!
   I'm hard as nails.
   I never fails!
I'm Bully Boy McCoy, avast!

I'm Bully Boy McCoy, ooh arrgh!
I navigates by sun an' by star.
   An' stealin' treasure?
   That's me pleasure!
I'm Bully Boy McCoy, ooh arrgh!

I'm Bully Boy McCoy, I be!
I'm sailing home to have me tea.
   I'm in a state,
   'Cause if I'm late—
My mommy will be cross with me!

WHEN A DINOSAUR DAD COMES HOME FROM WORK

Be nice to Dad when he comes home.
(Of course he'd never beat you!)
But if he's had a tiring day
He might just up and eat you!

EYE-DLE BOAST

If I should ever spy, clops,
A dirty great big cyclops,
I'd punch him in the eye, clops,
To show him who was boss!

DOWN IN THE JUNGLE

Down in the jungle,
  Living in a tree.
Better than a bungalow—
  It's free!

Down in the desert,
  Living in a tent.
Better than a mansion—
  No rent!

Down in the garbage dump,
  Living on a heap.
Better than a penthouse—
  Dirt cheap!

THE FORTH WORST POME WOT I EVER RITTED

Oh, the grand old Duke of York,

He had ten thousand men;

They all ran after the farmer's wife,

Who cut off their tails with a carving knife,

Did you ever see such a thing in your life?

Three bags full.

ANOTHER POEM TO SEND
TO YOUR WORST ENEMY

Dweeb, drip, softy, jerk,
Dope, sap, noodle, berk!
Fathead, bumpkin, duffer, mutt,
Loopy, potty, monkey nut!
Slimy crawler, teacher's pet.
Flat-foot-duck-toed-knock-kneed sweat!
Fleabag, snot-rag, waxy-ears.
Hope your acne never clears!
Airhead, doughbrain, pizzaface.
Reject from the human race!
Spotty stinkpot, silly fool.
Donkey, pinhead, pimply mule!
Blockhead, bonkers, soppy, wet—
Just how stupid can you get?

THERE'S A MONSTER IN THE NURSERY

There's a monster in the nursery.
    It's been asleep all day.
It's three o'clock in the morning
And the monster wants to play!

There's a monster in the nursery.
    What are we going to do?
Wash it off and change it
    'Cause the monster's done a poo!

There's a monster in the nursery.
    Its howls could wake the dead!
Get some milk and warm it
    'Cause the monster wants to be fed!

There's a monster in the nursery.
    Parents in a muddle.
What is it now? It's clean, it's fed—
    The monster wants a cuddle!

There's a monster in the nursery.
    It's enough to make you weep!
It's afternoon; it's time to play—
But the monster's fast asleep.

THE LITTLE MONSTER'S FAST ASLEEP!

FRANKENSTEIN'S MONSTER IS FINALLY DEAD!

Frankenstein's monster
    Is finally dead!
He was buried today
    And the will has been read.

The people were terrified
    Out of their wits,
So they sharpened their axes
    And chopped him in bits!

They cut off his arms
    And his legs and his head.
His innards? Just say that
    The dogs look well fed!

Oh, they buried him here
  And they buried him there.
They buried the monster
  Everywhere!

From this day on
  Sleep safe in your bed.
Frankenstein's monster
  Is finally dead.

Sons and daughters,
  Nephews and nieces,
The monster is dead —
  May he rest in pieces!

HEARTLESS

My heart belongs to Frankenstein.
What more can I say?
I've fallen in love with Frankenstein:
He's stolen my heart away!

TAKING AFTER GRANDMOTHER

My late-lamented grandmama
Loved flying, so I've heard.
Perhaps that would explain
My slight resemblance to a bird.

THE OOZE-ZOMBIE FROM
THE SLIME-PITS OF GRUNGE!

I only suggested that he
Should use a mouthwash
And maybe brush his teeth
Once in a while.
"That's no reason to bite
My head off!" I said
As he bit my head off.

THE DOOM MERCHANT

Down in the dumps,
At the end of the road to Rack and Ruin
And just beyond Hope,
Jeremiah, the Doom Merchant, has opened for business.
(And a sorry business it is too!)

He sits in his shop painting a gloomy picture of a sea of troubles.
He is wrapped in a wet blanket.
He has cold feet.
Perched on his shoulder is a Nagging Doubt.

He has Fate in store.

He has a shelf full of Bad Tidings.
He sells Dashed Hopes and Storm Warnings.
He sells Misfortunes (they come in threes).
He sells Umbrellas (to be set aside for a rainy day).
He sells Hats (labeled, "On your head be it").
He sells Traps (to keep the wolf from the door).
He sells Life Jackets and Safety Nets (without guarantees).
He sells Handkerchiefs (to wipe away the bitter tears).

On the Doom Merchant's shop window is a permanent sign:
"CLOSING DOWN SALE —
THE END OF THE WORLD IS NIGH."

MAKING FRIENDS WITH FRANKENSTEIN

When I am feeling lonely,
For Igor I will send.
We'll go to my laboratory
And we will make a friend!

ODE TO THE INVISIBLE MAN

OGRE MY DEAD BODY! (The Ogre's Song)

Wen I is famished, feelin pekky,
I eat hewmin beens for brekky!
Brekky, brekky, feelin pekky,
I eat hewmin beens for brekky!

Wen I is ungry for me lunsh,
It's hewmin beens I luvs ta crunch!
Crunch, crunch, luvs ta crunch,
Hewmin beens for me lunsh!

Wen I is clammin for me dinner,
I catch a hewmin been an skin 'er!
Skin 'er, skin 'er for me dinner,
Catch a hewmin been an skin 'er!

An wen I needs a midnite snack,
Heer them hewmin bones go CRACK!
CRACK, CRACK, midnite snack,
Heer them hewmin bones go CRACK!

Yah, boo, hiss
To all of you!
My best friend
Is nine foot two!

THE WILD BILL HICKOK BIRD

Here's news for ornithologists,
I thought you'd like to know:
It concerns a tiny island
In the Gulf of Mexico.

It may be hard to swallow,
But you'll have to take my word.
Explorers have discovered
An amazing little bird.

It's called the Wild Bill Hickok Bird.
We think it is unique.
It fires rock-hard hazelnuts
From its barrel beak!

The island's population,
According to my spies,
Are all retired cowboys —
You won't believe your eyes!

The cowboys carry gun belts
And—I know this sounds absurd—
Instead of guns and pistols
Use the Wild Bill Hickok Bird!

The rootin', tootin' cowboy,
You should see the way he struts,
Has no ammunition problem 'cause
The island's full of nuts!

And at a recent gunfight
Guess what was overheard.
They didn't say, "Go fer ya gun!"
They said, "Go fer ya BIRD!"

So if you go there bird-watching,
I really think it's best,
Take your big binoculars
And bullet-proof your vest!

THE LADY IN LOVE

There was a lady loved a swine:
"Piggy-wig, wilt thou be mine?
I'll dress you up in silks so fine."
"Grunt!" said the pig.

"I'll build for thee a silver sty.
I'll cook for thee a pigeon pie.
On goose-down feathers wilt thou lie."
"Oink!" said the pig.

"I'll sew and wash and clean and bake.
I'll make for thee a wedding cake.
If you say no my heart will break."
"Snort!" said the pig.

"I'll steal for thee. I'd go to jail.
I will be true — I'll never fail.
O wilt thou have me, curly tail?"
"What's the catch?" said the pig.

SQUELCH!

I am a dainty Brontosaurus,
  Skipping through the meadow.
Oops-a-daisy! Pardon me!
  Must watch where I tread-o!

(Silly place to have a picnic anyway!)

FRUIT BATS IN THE ATTIC!

Fruit bats in the attic;
    Armadillos in the hall.
Piranhas in the bathtub;
    Iguanas up the wall.

Camels in the bedroom;
    Alligators in the sink.
Impalas in the cellar.
    What on earth will people think?

Lions in the cupboards;
    Anacondas on the stair.
Pandas on the balcony.
    Mom's pulling out her hair.

Koalas in the closet.
    The shed? Two kangaroos!
In Granny's room, an elephant—
    (Granny's got the blues!).

Mother said to Father,
    "This has got to stop!
You must not bring your work home
    From the taxidermy shop!"

DEAD RINGER

Death in the steeple!
Tell the people!
I've a hunch I knew him well!
Dead as a dodo!
Quasimodo!
It's his face that rings a bell!

You must be jealous of me!
I'm as handsome as can be.
  My IQ's high;
  It's obvious why.
You must be jealous of me!

You must be jealous of me!
I'm over six foot three.
  The girls all sigh
  When I pass by.
You must be jealous of me!

You must be jealous of me!
I'm fabulous, yippee!
  I must confess,
  I'm modest, yes.
You must be jealous of me!

You must be jealous of me!
I'm special, you'll agree.
  My jokes are funny.
  I've heaps of money.
You must be jealous of me!

You must be jealous of me!
Quite understandably.
  I've the fastest car.
  I'm a superstar.
You must be jealous of me!

You must be jealous of me!
Yet you don't seem to be.
  I can't see why —
  I'm a wonderful guy.
You MUST be jealous of me!

IT WAS A DAY LIKE ANY OTHER IN FISHTOWN

"Spare a penny, mister?" said the sea urchin.

"Neigh!" said the sea horse.

"Outta my way!" said the mussel.

"Hallelujah!" said the angelfish.

"You'll get nothing from me," said the clam.

"Weeee!" said the flying fish.

"Woof!" said the dogfish.

"Shocking!" said the electric eel.

"Do you think I'm made of money?" said the goldfish.

IF I HAD A MONSTER

If I had a monster,
I'll tell you what I'd do.
I'd starve it for a week
And then I'd set it on you!

IF A BIRD SINGS IN A BIRDCAGE

If a bird sings in a birdcage,
Well, I haven't any doubt,
He isn't singing out of joy,
He's singing, "LET ME OUT!"

A POUND OF GUMMY BABIES

A pound of gummy babies,
  Just for me!
Slobber, chomp, slurp, gulp!
  Tee-hee-hee!

A pound of gummy babies,
  Eat my fill!
Slobber, chomp, slurp, gulp!
  I feel ill!

A pound of gummy babies,
  Ate too quick!
Slobber, chomp, slurp, gulp!
  I feel sick!

A pound of gummy babies,
  Oh, dear me!
Slobber,
  chomp,
   slurp,
  gulp!

BLEARRGGHHOOOWOURGHH!!!

THE SHADY CHARACTER

There's a shady character following me!
Who can the shady character be?

He silently slithers,
Dresses in black.
He's normally hiding
Behind my back!
The strange thing is,
When the sun isn't out,
The shady character's never about!
When it's raining or snowing
Or cloudy or gray,
The shady character stays away!
But he comes back at night
As I walk down the street,
Sometimes long; sometimes short;
Sometimes under my feet!
Passing from streetlight to streetlight I find
He's sometimes in front of me,
Sometimes behind!

There's a shady character
Following me.
Who can the shady
Character be?

MY LITTLE BROTHER IS REALLY WEIRD!

My little brother
Is really weird.
He's up and gone
And grown a beard!

Oh, the embarrassment,
Oh, the disgrace —
The neighbors call him
FUNGUS FACE!

Easy!

THAT'S IMPOSSIBLE, MISS!

"Nothing is impossible!"
Said the teacher with a hiss.
"How about a cross-eyed
Cyclops, Miss?"

THE UGLY CUSTOMER

A fancy car screeched to a stop.
A lady rushed into the shop,
(A beauty parlor, New York State),
Said, "Make it quick, I've got a date!
What'll it take to make me pretty,
The cutest girl in New York City?"

The shop went quiet, not a sound,
The staff and clients turned around,
And with a smile said the beautician,
"Madam, I am no magician.
No offense, but since you ask,
Perhaps I might suggest a mask!"

I'VE LOST MY HEAD!

The phantom standing
At my bedroom door
Handed me a note
With a grizzly paw:

"Sorry to disturb you
In your bed,
But could you help?
I've lost my head!"

I should have shouted
For my mom and dad,
But his shoulders drooped
And he looked so sad.

We searched the house,
Looked everywhere;
At last we found it
Under the stair.

He picked it up
And screwed it on,
Said, "Ah, that's better!"
And then was gone.

He upped and left me,
Walked through a wall;
Manners of a pig,
Didn't thank me at all!

I went upstairs
And back to bed;
I didn't get angry,
I kept my head.

But I'm losing patience
With that freak—
It's the fifteenth time
It's happened this week!

If it happens again,
I know what I'll do.
I'll stick it back on
With super glue!

A CYCLOPS CAN NEVER BE FRIENDS WITH ANOTHER

A cyclops can never
Be friends with another.
Be they auntie or uncle
Or sister or brother
Or nephews or nieces
Or father or mother—
They never see eye to eye!

A cyclops will argue
And say black is white,
The sun is the moon,
Up is down, day is night.
Coffee is tea,
Hot is cold, wrong is right—
They never see eye to eye!

When babies, they'll argue
Their diapers are clean.
If you point out a whale
They will say "a sardine!"
When it comes to TV,
Then they get really mean—
They never see eye to eye!

When the weather is fine
They will say that it's raining.
They'll fight, though they're full,
Over food that's remaining.
If something is boring
They'll say entertaining—
They never see eye to eye!

If one says, "Good morning,"
They'll answer, "Good night!"
If one says it's dull,
The response is, "Too bright!"
The commonest phrase is:
"DO YOU WANNA FIGHT?"—
They never see eye to eye!

I'm talking big!

I'm talking huge!

I'm talking enormous, immense,

Tremendous!

I'm talking hulking, towering,

Titanic, mountainous!

I'm talking maximum, massive

Stupendous, gigantic, monumental!

I'm talking fantastic, fabulous,

Incredible, unbelievable, mammoth,

Vast!

I'm talking astronomical, mighty,

Monstrous, universal, colossal,

Magnificent, galactical!

I'm talking BIG!

THE ALIEN VISITOR

When the alien visitor
Visits our school,
Please be polite to him,
Don't play the fool.

His skin may be purple
Or orange or blue,
But you must not be rude,
Whatever you do.

He may be all hairy;
He may have no hair.
Don't ogle or gawk —
I forbid you to stare!

He may be enormous,
He may be quite small,
But don't call him, "Shorty!"
That won't do at all.

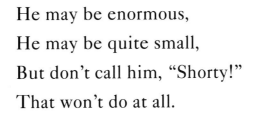

He may have two heads
But you mustn't make fun.
Remember that two heads
Are better than one.

He may well give off
A peculiar smell.
The first one to shout,
"What a stink!" I'll expel!

Speak when you're spoken to,
Don't be a pest.
Try to remember
That he is our guest.

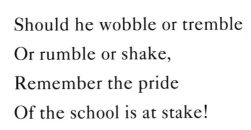

Should he wobble or tremble
Or rumble or shake,
Remember the pride
Of the school is at stake!

Should he shudder or gargle
Or blargle or bubble,
Any giggling, Lawson,
And you'll be in trouble!

Giggle
Giggle

So behave yourselves, children,
And don't be alarmed.
(You can't be too careful —
He may well be armed!)

Quiet a moment!
Here is a note.
It's written in alien.
It says, and I quote:

"BOING, YARP PALARVA
BEEP PLARGLE SPLING SPLOFF!"
He's seen our school photo —
It's frightened him off!

BOING, YARP PALARVA!

The visit is canceled.
Forget what I've said.
The alien is visiting
Venus instead!

AN ABOMINABLE VERSE

Have you noticed how the yeti
Rhymes so neatly with spaghetti?
It is, alas, a waste of ink
To search for any missing link!

I LOVE YOU 'CAUSE

I love you 'cause
   Your hair is fine and silky.
I love you 'cause
   Your eyes are black as pitch.
I love you 'cause
   Your skin is smooth and milky.
But most of all I love you
   'Cause you're rich!

JEKYLL AND HYDE PARK

Come with me and see our park —
We'll pay a visit after dark.
(There's a full moon tonight!)

Hiding deep within the shrubbery,
See the creature soft and rubbery.
(He'd love to eat — I mean — meet you!)

At the bottom of the slide
Waits a mouth that's three feet wide.
(Why not have a try?)

Beneath the bandstand in the slime,
A monster made by Frankenstein.
(May he rest in pieces!)

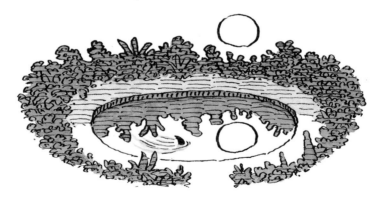

Don't go rowing! Disembark!
You may meet the great white shark.
(Jaws truly!)

Turn over!

In the fountain, watching us,
A googly-eyeballed octopus.
(He doesn't eat meat — only vegetarians!)

In the sandbox, making trouble,
Seven witches, hubble, bubble.
(Sandwitches!)

Have you ever met a zombie?
'Evening, Mr. Abercrombie.
(Poor thing looks dead on his feet!)

What's a werewolf like the most?
Answer: human beans on toast.
(A howler!)

Gorilla? Dress? Something's wrong!
Pleased to meet you, Mrs. Kong.
(Nice outfit, Your Majesty!)

Floral border, spick and span,
Watch out for the bogeyman.
(He gets right up my nose!)

See the creature mean and sweaty?
That's a Himalayan yeti.
(What an abominable smell!)

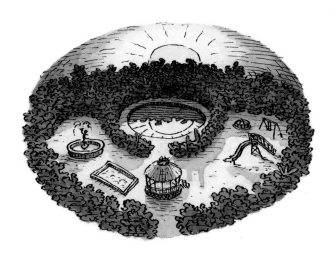

But don't you worry, never fear—
At dawn the monsters disappear!
(Like your granny's teeth, they
only come out at night!)

THE CROCODILE WITH TOOTHACHE

In all my life (I'm eighty-four!),
    The saddest thing I ever saw
Was in the swamps of Uskabore—
    The crocodile with toothache.

He whined and wailed; he bit his fist.
    He called for an anesthetist.
But tell me, how does one assist
    The crocodile with toothache?

When they heard the awful sound,
    The people came from miles around
And on the riverbank they found
    The crocodile with toothache!

Then, from the people standing there,
    Emerged a hero, bold and fair.
He said, "Stand back and I'll repair
    The crocodile with toothache!"

The hero bold said, "Open wide!"
   The crocodile looked up and smiled
And said, "Why don't you come inside
   The crocodile with toothache!"

He swallowed GULP! to our disgust,
   And swam off laughing, fit to bust.
The lesson here is never trust
   The crocodile with toothache!

THERE WAS AN OLD WOMAN

There was an old woman
    Who lived in a shoe.
The giant who owned it
    Said, "What can I do?
My foot it has blisters.
    I can't hardly walk."
The woman said, "HOP IT,
    I've no time to talk!"

Can't you see I'm busy?

COUSIN NEVILLE

Speak of the devil,
Meet cousin Neville!

SOPHIE CHARLOTTE WYATT-WYATT

Sophie Charlotte Wyatt-Wyatt
Wouldn't eat a proper diet.
All she'd eat were snails and slugs.
(She bought them by the pint in jugs!)
She grew to twelve, then through her teens,
Not tasting fish or fowl or greens.
It hasn't done her any harm;
She's small and pretty — full of charm.
Though Sophie Charlotte I adore,
She has the odd annoying flaw:
She's very shy, stays in her shell.
She's also rather slow, as well.
And when we're walking in the park,
(At my insistence, after dark!)
Miss Wyatt-Wyatt is inclined
To leave a trail of slime behind!

ANCIENT EGYPTIAN JOKE

Father's wrapped in bandages:
Head, arms, legs, and tummy.
Perhaps an explanation's due —
My daddy is a mummy!

TRANSYLVANIA DREAMING

In the middle of the night
When you're safe in bed
And the doors are locked
And the cats are fed
And it's much too bright
And sleep won't come
And there's something wrong
And you want your mom
And you hear a noise
And you see a shape
And it looks like a bat
Or a man in a cape
And you dare not breathe
And your heart skips a beat
And you're cold as ice
From your head to your feet
And you say a prayer
And you swear to be good
And you'd run for your life
If you only could
And your eyes are wide
And stuck on stalks
As the thing in black

Toward you walks
And the room goes dark
And you faint clean away
And you don't wake up
Till the very next day . . .

And you open your eyes
And the sun is out
And you jump out of bed
And you sing and shout,
"It was only a dream!"
And you dance around the room
And your heart is as light
As a helium balloon
And your mom rushes in
And says, "Hold on a sec . . .

What are those two little
Holes in your neck?"

ASSAULT AND FLATTERY

I'm on my way to school, I am,
When someone knocked me down.
It was that brute named Hoolihan,
A bully of renown.

That ugly brute named Hoolihan
Said, "Sorry, but you see,
I really can't abide a boy
Who's handsomer than me!"

PROFESSOR BLINKER

Professor Blinker
Worked so hard.
He built a bomb
In his backyard.

He lit the fuse
And stood well back,
But not quite far enough,
Alack!

The bomb went off:

BANG!

Oh, dear me.
Professor Blinker,
R.I.P.

The Bomb

The Professor

MONKEY NUTS

I bought a little monkey
In nineteen eighty-two.
The trouble was he grew and grew
And grew and grew and grew!

Up and up and up he went,
Right up to the ceiling.
Perhaps you can imagine how
My family was feeling!

We took out all the ceilings.
We took out all the doors.
We took out all the inside walls.
We took out all the floors.

In came the doctor.
In came the nurse.
In came the lady . . .
(Oops, sorry—wrong poem!)

I guess the birth certificate
Showed there was something wrong,
For in the space marked, "Father's name"
It simply said, "KING KONG"!

SHARK IN THE SHOWER

The shark in the shower
Sings a little song.
I have to get to work today;
I hope he won't be long.

GHOSTS AND SPIRITS

Ghosts and spirits, once a year,
Like to give themselves a scare.
Just for fun at Christmastime
They like to see a phantomime!

OH, YES IT IS!

Ladies and Gentlemen,
Roll up and see
The special free offer today.
You won't pay a thing
On the scaremonger's stall.
I'm giving it all away!

I'll give you the jitters,
I'll give you the jumps,
I'll make your knees tremble and knock!
I'll give you the shivers,
I'll give you a turn,
I'll give you a terrible shock!

Oh, I'll give you a fright
And I'll give you a start!
I'll give you a nasty surprise!
I'll give you the willies,
I'll give you the creeps.
You'll never believe your eyes!

So, Ladies and Gentlemen,
Step right this way.
Roll up and listen to me!
Ladies and Gentlemen—
Just for today—
I'll give you a scare for free!

THE GIANT PIG

The giant pig strolled into town
   And on the butcher's shop sat down.
He said, "Good morning," with a frown
   To Mr. Bones the Butcher.

He'd heard a rumor, there'd been talk,
   The butcher had been selling pork,
And so he thought he'd take a walk
   To Mr. Bones the Butcher.

The shop was wrecked, a pile of rubble.
   A certain person's in big trouble.
Listen to him squeak and bubble!
   Mr. Bones the Butcher.

The pig stood up, said, "Toodle-oo,
   Good-bye, farewell, ta ta, adieu."
Then glaring down said, "Shame on you!"
   To Mr. Bones the Butcher.

Lesson given, lesson taken.
   Unless I'm very much mistaken
That's the last time you'll sell bacon,
   Mr. Bones the Butcher!

A FAREWELL TO DRACULA

So long,
Sucker!

INDEX